Swami Vivekananda
Edward T. Sturdy

Narada Bhakti Sutras

The Path of Love for God

ed. and with an introduction by
Gabriele Ebert

Bibliografische Informationen der Deutschen Bibliothek
Die Deutsche Bibliothek verzeichnet diese Publikation in
der Deutschen Nationalbibliografie; detaillierte bibliografische Daten sind im Internet über http://dnb.ddb.de abrufbar.

Edward T. Sturdy: Narada Sutra: An Inquiry into Love
(Bhakti-Jijnasa), London, 1896
Vivekananda: Narada Bhakti Sutras, in: Notes of Class
Talks and Lectures, Complete Works VI
Vivekananda: Inspired Talks, 24. June 1895, in: Complete
Works VII
Herstellung und Verlag: BoD – Books on Demand,
Norderstedt
ISBN: 9783757847432
Book cover: probably Narada, from the collection of the
British Museum, Wikimedia Commons, 19th century

Contents

FSC
www.fsc.org
MIX
Papier aus ver-
antwortungsvollen
Quellen
Paper from
responsible sources
FSC® C105338

Introduction

Sutras are guides, aphorisms, short instructive sentences. The Narada Bhakti Sutras contains 84 such aphorisms about the love of God, the Bhakti-marga (path of love of God) or Bhakti-Yoga, which is one of the four yoga paths in India, along with Karma-Yoga (the yoga of action), Jnana-Yoga (the yoga of knowledge) and Raja-Yoga (the classical, royal yoga). They are considered a standard work, to which there are many translations from Sanskrit into English and commentaries.

Narada, to whom the Bhakti Sutras are attributed, is a sage from Indian mythology, known in the Hindu tradition as a traveling musician and storyteller. He delivers messages and enlightening wisdom to the sages and gods, traveling to distant worlds and realms. Often depicted with a vina and a khartal, he is considered a master of ancient musical instruments and glorifies Vishnu with his devotional songs. He is considered to be one of the sons created by the spirit of Brahma, the creator god, or, according to another tradition, the son of the sage Kashyapa. According to the Bhagavata Purana, he is descended from the mind of Hari (Vishnu). He appears in a number of Hindu texts, especially in the Mahabharata and the Ramayana as well as in narratives of the Puranas.[1]

A chronological classification for the origin of Narada's sutras cannot be determined. The story of their origin is told by Swami Sivananda in the introduction to his translation: "One day Narada went to the Ashram [of Vyasa] in the course of his wanderings. Sri Vyasa welcomed the Rishi with due rites and said, 'Man seeks freedom, etc. But without devotion it is dry. Devotion is the only way for attaining salvation. All the others have importance only in so far as they are auxiliary to it. I humbly ask you to explain to me the virtue of devotion.'"[2]

Narada then explained bhakti in the form of these 84 sutras.

Swami Vivekananda (1863-1902), the famous disciple of Ramakrishna who brought all four kinds of yoga and Vedanta, the teaching of non-duality, to the West, was in London in the fall of 1895, where he wanted to establish a Vedanta center. He was assisted by Edward Toronto Sturdy (1860-1957), a former theosophist who had spent some time in India and became his devoted disciple. Vivekananda, in turn, helped him with

---

[1] s. https://www.vyasaonline.com/encyclopedia/narada/ (22.7.2023)

[2] Swami Sivananda: Narada Bhakit Sutras, Uttarakhand, 2008, p. 7: https://gurudevsivananda.org/Narada_Bhakti_Sutras.pdf (22.7.2023)

his study and translation of the Narada Bhakti Sutras from Sanskrit and also with a commentary on them that clearly bears Vivekananda's signature. Sturdy published this work in 1896 under the title "Narada Sutra: An Inquiry into Love." This book contains a general introduction and an article on Vivekananda in the appendix, which have not been included here.

In addition, a freer translation of the Narada Bhakti Sutras by Vivekananda has survived in his Complete Works, which I have included. However, some verses are missing.

In the summer of 1895, Vivekananda and a small group of students spent several weeks in Thousand Island Park, a village on Wellesley Island, one of the largest islands in the Thousand Island group on the St. Lawrence River in New York State, where he gave daily classes. His lecture on June 24 was on the Narada Bhakti Sutras. Like the other lectures, it was also transcribed.

The Narada Bhakti Sutras are still current. The same statements about the love to God are found in all religions, including Christianity. God is love – this is said everywhere. As love, God, whether personal or impersonal, can be understood and experienced by all.

Gabriele Ebert

Vivekananda: Narada Bhakti Sutras

(A free translation by Swami Vivekananda;
Complete Works VI[3])

Chapter I

1. Bhakti is intense love for God.

2. It is the nectar of love;

3. Getting which man becomes perfect, immortal, and satisfied for ever;

4. Getting which man desires no more, does not become jealous of anything, does not take pleasure in vanities:

5. Knowing which man becomes filled with spirituality, becomes calm, and finds pleasure only in God.

6. It cannot be used to fill any desire, itself being the check to all desires.

7. Sannyasa is giving up both the popular and the scriptural forms of worship.

8. The Bhakti-Sannyasin is the one whose whole soul goes unto God, and whatever militates against love to God, he rejects.

---

[3] Swami Vivekananda: Complete Works: http://ramakrishnavivekananda.info/vivekananda/complete_works.htm (22.7.2023)

9. Giving up all other refuge, he takes refuge in God.

10. Scriptures are to be followed as long as one's life has not become firm;

11. Or else there is danger of doing evil in the name of liberty.

12. When love becomes established, even social forms are given up, except those which are necessary for the preservation of life.

13. There have been many definitions of love, but Narada gives these as the signs of love: When all thoughts, all words, and all deeds are given up unto the Lord, and the least forgetfulness of God makes one intensely miserable, then love has begun.

14. As the Gopis had it –

15. Because, although worshipping God as their lover, they never forgot his God-nature;

16. Otherwise they would have committed the sin of unchastity.

17. This is the highest form of love, because there is no desire of reciprocity, which desire is in all human love.

Chapter II

1. Bhakti is greater than Karma, greater than Jnana, greater than Yoga (Raja-Yoga), because Bhakti itself

is its result, because Bhakti is both the means and the end (fruit).

2. As a man cannot satisfy his hunger by simple knowledge or sight of food, so a man cannot be satisfied by the knowledge or even the perception of God until love comes; therefore love is the highest.

Chapter III

1. These, however, the Masters have said about Bhakti:

2. One who wants this Bhakti must give up sense enjoyments and even the company of people.

3. Day and night he must think about Bhakti and nothing else.

4. (He must) go where they sing or talk of God.

5. The principal cause of Bhakti is the mercy of a great (or free) soul.

6. Meeting with a great soul is hard to obtain, and never fails to save the soul.

7. Through the mercy of God we get such Gurus.

8. There is no difference between Him and His (own) ones.

9. Seek, therefore, for this.

10. Evil company is always to be shunned;

11. Because it leads to lust and anger, illusion, forgetfulness of the goal, destruction of the will (lack of perseverance), and destruction of everything.

12. These disturbances may at first be like ripples, but evil company at last makes them like the sea.

13. He gets across Maya who gives up all attachment, serves the great ones, lives alone, cuts the bondages of this world, goes beyond the qualities of nature, and depends upon the Lord for even his living.

14. He who gives up the fruits of work, he who gives up all work and the dualism of joy and misery, who gives up even the scriptures, gets that unbroken love for God.

15. He crosses this river and helps others to cross it.

Chapter IV

1. The nature of love is inexpressible.

2. As the dumb man cannot express what he tastes, but his actions betray his feelings, so man cannot express this love in words, but his actions betray it.

3. In some rare persons it is expressed.

4. Beyond all qualities, all desires, ever increasing, unbroken, the finest perception is love.

5. When a man gets this love, he sees love everywhere he hears love everywhere, he talks love everywhere, he thinks love everywhere.

6. According to the qualities or conditions, this love manifests itself differently.

7. The qualities are: Tamas (dullness, heaviness), Rajas (restlessness, activity), Sattva (serenity, purity); and the conditions are: Arta (afflicted), Artarthi (wanting something), Jijnasu (searching truth), Jnani, (knower).

8. Of these the latter are higher than the preceding ones.

9. Bhakti is the easiest way of worship.

10. It is its own proof and does not require any other.

11. Its nature is peace and perfect bliss.

12. Bhakti never seeks to injure anyone or anything not even the popular modes of worship.

13. Conversation about lust, or doubt of God or about one's enemies must not be listened to.

14. Egotism, pride, etc. must be given up.

15. If those passions cannot be controlled, place them upon God, and place all your actions on Him.

16. Merging the trinity of Love, Lover, and Beloved, worship God as His eternal servant, His eternal bride – thus love is to be made unto God.

Chapter V

1. That love is highest which is concentrated upon God.

2. When such speak of God, their voices stick in their throats, they cry and weep; and it is they who give holy places their holiness; they make good works, good books better, because they are permeated with God.

3. When a man loves God so much, his forefathers rejoice, the gods dance, and the earth gets a Master!

4. To such lovers there is no difference of caste, sex, knowledge, form, birth, or wealth;

5. Because they are all God's.

6. Arguments are to be avoided;

7. Because there is no end to them, and they lead to no satisfactory result.

8. Read books treating of this love, and do deeds which increase it.

9. Giving up all desires of pleasure and pain, gain and loss, worship God day and night. Not a moment is to be spent in vain.

10. Ahimsa (non-killing), truthfulness, purity, mercy, and godliness are always to be kept.

11. Giving up all other thoughts, the whole mind should day and night worship God. Thus being worshipped day and night, He reveals Himself and makes His worshippers feel Him.

12. In past, present, and future, Love is greatest!

Thus following the ancient sages, we have dared to preach the doctrine of *Love*, without fearing the jeers of the world.

Edward T. Sturdy:
Narada Sutra or Inquiry into Love (Bhakti)

Edward T. Sturdy, ca. 1902, Vivekananda in London, 1895

1. We will now explain Love (bhakti).

2. Its nature is extreme devotion (prema-rupa) to some one.

3. Love is immortal (amṛta-rupa).

We are met at the outset in these verses with two words: bhakti and prema. The first has often been translated by "faith" and thus confusion has arisen and the term been identified with the Western doctrine of faith, with which it has nothing to do. It signifies devotion, love, loyalty to something higher than oneself, mingled with an element of respect, reverence and worship.

Prema, on the other hand, signifies intense devotion, the love and loyalty of an equal to an equal; and is a higher form. It is the stage in which the devotee stands to Deity in the light of beloved and lover, to be followed later by a complete identity of the two.

Although bhakti may often be used in the sense of prema yet the reverse is never found. For example:

"I am the same amidst all beings, for me none is hateful, none lovable, but they who worship me with love (*bhakti*) are in me, and I also in them." Bh. Gita, IX, 29

Here lover and beloved are signified, and *bhakti* stands for prema. All through the Narada Sutra, then, bhakti stands for para (excessive) bhakti, and this is the same as prema. Hence the second verse identifies bhakti with prema, so that its lesser meanings of worship, as with ritual, etc., may not confuse the reader. For instance, love takes the "nature of extreme devotion" of one to another here in the objective world – in the world of mortals. But Love itself is never seen. Its manifestations only are seen. "Love is immortal."

Love is one of the definitions or methods by which the finite and mortal mind tries to express its conception of its essential and eternal nature. Through the veil of the brain and senses this appears as separate from itself, as a divine principle, which illumines the mind with a ray of itself ("Love is God.")

This conception of the abstract principle of Love as lover is an enormous help in the ascent which the mind is at length destined to make to the ultimate disclosure, the last words that can be spoken, that "thou thyself art THAT." It is the natural process through which man passes, and the various conceptions of religion show its different phases up to the highest and ultimate expression, the Advaita Vedanta, which recognises no duality, nothing apart from the Self anywhere.

"I become the raiser without delay from the ocean of birth and death of those who have entered into me through their minds." Bh. Gita, XII, 7

4. Obtaining which man becomes perfect, becomes immortal, becomes satisfied.

5. And obtaining which he desires nothing, grieves not, hates not, does not delight (in sensuous objects), makes no effort (for selfish ends).

6. Knowing which he becomes intoxicated (with joy), transfixed, and rejoices in the Self.

When man has united himself with Love he has identified himself with perfection, for he has come into harmony with that in which there is no flaw.

He becomes immortal by virtue of that union.

He is satisfied, for he has given all and asks for nothing in return. He cannot suffer nor hate, for he has identified himself with all life, and for him separation, injury, "mine" and "thine" and all those fallacies by which we are bound, cease to exist.

How can he delight in sensuous objects which require attachment to a concrete, selfish personality? For what should one work who sees himself everywhere?

It is only by some small gleam of happiness that even the most oppressed, the most miserable of men maintain existence. This happiness increased as Love is realised. Even without wisdom who has not at some time experienced pleasure? But it faded out quickly, because it was merely the realisation of a desire or gratification of the will; and the desire and realisation were both of something transient. The gratified wish and the happiness attending it soon fade into the grey of the past and seem then no theme for aught but regret, or, at the best, reflection.

But he who has realised Love has found the source of all happiness: of happiness which cannot fade, because its object is imperishable. There is no name that adequately describes this state. To do so words must be used which speak by contrast – mattah, mad, intoxicated.

"He recognised that Happiness is Brahman; from Happiness, indeed, all these creatures are born; when born they live through Happiness; when they depart, they enter into Happiness." Tait. Up., Ill, 6.

Self – Atman – is the philosophical word which tries to define the same abstraction which he who treads the path of devotion calls Love. "He rejoices in the Self," common to all manifestation now identical with himself.

7. It (Love) cannot be made to fulfil desires, for its nature is renunciation.

8. Renunciation is the giving up of ritual and worldly affairs.

9. Exclusive devotion to Love and indifference to everything opposed to it.

10. Exclusive devotion is abandoning all other refuges (but Love).

11. And in worldly affairs and in the Scriptures, following whatever is in conformity with it.

12. Let the injunctions of Scriptures be followed until conviction has become firm.

13. Otherwise there is danger of falling.

14. Worldly usages are also to be recognised until then, but eating and other necessary bodily activities will remain as long as the body is retained.

If any doubt remains as to the nature of the love of which the Narada Sutra treats, as to whether it refers to human passion or that other wonderful attribute, divine in its nature, which man can make manifest within himself, Sutra 7 sets this at rest. The very nature of this Love is renunciation.

Love may be divided threefold.

1. Where the only motive is to receive pleasure – to take all and give nothing.

2. Where there is exchange, and the loving depends upon being loved – "I love thee because thou lovest me."

3. Where there is unconditional devotion, the giving everything and seeking nothing, no recognition, no return.

In the first category must be placed the sensualist; in the second, the ordinary human love between men and women, or between friends; sometimes this is dashed with some small fragrance of the third. He who holds only the third is the true Bhakta. He alone stands on the verge of himself, being merged entirely in Love – in Deity – and in the non-recognition anywhere of "I" and "thou." To him it is all "I" or all "thou," with no division either between himself and others, or between himself and God.

Renunciation is said to be the giving up of ritual and worldly affairs. Ritual is performed to gain some advantage, here or hereafter. Worldly affairs are followed for the gain of prosperity or ambition. All these objects are foreign to Love; but they may be instruments used for the good of the world, and are then "in conformity with" Love.

They cannot be given up suddenly; in that case the renunciation is far more likely to end in downfall, to relapse into licence, to result in carelessness in regard to sacred things – in short, deeper bondage rather than in freedom.

Only the strong can be free: only the perfect lover can cast away all the protections which long ages of human suffering and experience have built up as armour for the individual and society. As long as man has a body, so long will it require food, rest and protection from heat, cold, etc. There is a warning applied here against false asceticism, which produces an intensification of selfish egotism; does not reduce it.

He who loves equally everywhere need seek no asceticism: it will seek him as long as he has a coin to spend, a loaf to divide or a coat to give. And it will remain with him until the end. Care of the body must not be ignored, and the degree of advance towards true Knowledge and Love depends upon the attitude of the mind, as to whether the body be looked upon as "'my body" or merely as "this body." Perfect chastity and the intensely positive state which is produced by constant control of all angry, envious, ambitious or sensuous thoughts reacts upon the physical frame. There is no loss of force in nature. The will turned back from dissipating itself upon these external states reasserts itself in a superior manifestation as ojas – power, vigour, fire, splendour, applied to everything that is undertaken. By ojas, the bhakta, the jnani and the tapasvi – the lover of God, the man who has attained perfect discernment, and the ascetic – defy alike the biting winds and snows of the mountain height and the scorching sun of the plains and deserts.

15. Definitions of love are now given according to different opinions.

16. Vyasa says it is devotion to worship.

17. Garga says it is devotion to hearing about Atman.

18. Sandilya says it is the unbroken feeling of the Universal Self in one's own self.

19. But Narada says it is surrendering all actions to God, and feeling the greatest misery in forgetting God.

20. It is indeed thus.

Four definitions are now given of Love. The first two may be said to be ritualistic devotion. The last two represent the two great schools of dualists and non-dualists. Narada Sutra is dualistic, Sandilya Sutra is non-dualistic.

The first claims a Deity external to the soul and eternally separate.

The second recognises one Eternal Self only as manifesting in all creatures: these apparently separate existences may be produced by limitation of Love in them and the production of selfishness. When the fulness of Love is reached, the recognition of "One without a second" is attained. As long as there is no desire for Love, which dissolves all limitations, there is individual selfish life following life, with the attendant miseries of birth, growth, old age, decay and death. There is no peace, no goal for those who do not learn to love: they beat backward and forward on the storm-tossed ocean of separation called the world, striving ever for the most futile and ephemeral of things, for personal and separate existence, for self-solicitude. Alas! what misery is theirs. Such striving fulfils not even the average conceptions of ethics and philosophy.

Self-affirmation is death; self-negation is life eternal.

Sankaracarya, the great expounder of the non-dualistic system, has pointed out that the teaching of non-duality comes as an amplification of other doctrines, not as a contradiction of them.

He, then, who holds this doctrine, can look with perfect sympathy and patience upon those who still need, or still see, a Deity, or deities, in nature, separate from themselves.

The mind cannot always dwell in the highest abstractions: it can then drop back with safety to the conception of itself as separate from Deity. Upon so doing, in reality, the centre of consciousness being lowered, the mind again takes on the form of "I" and sees what is beyond this conception, the Changeless Self, God, as now apparently outside and beyond itself – as non-I. From this standpoint it strives for complete surrender to the Divine Will, as slave, as servant, or as lover. With complete acquiescence there comes complete identity. In complete love there is no room for "I" and "thou."

21. As was the case with the shepherdesses of Vraja.

22. Not even there can imputation be made that the knowledge of the Great Self was forgotten.

23. Devoid of that it would have been the love of paramours.

24. There is not in this love (of paramours) happiness in the other's happiness only.

This reference is to the playing of Krishna with the shepherdesses as described in the Vishnu Purana and elsewhere. Perhaps no Hindu allegory has been so aspersed: it has been made by some few debased people of India, as similar allegories have in other countries, an excuse for licence under the cloak of religion. It has been used by the ignorant, by missionaries and others, as a weapon of hostile criticism against Hindu religions. We may safely assert that none of these have read the original, but merely sought some means to destroy other people's religion in order to advocate their own. Time might better be employed in pointing out the original intention of the allegory by which they would elevate both themselves and the people with whom they come in contact. By taking the other attitude they confirm the pariah in his ignorance, stimulate his resentment, and stand as the enemies of Krishna the Divine. Love is one, whether it be called that of Christ, Krishna, or any other individualised expression of

Truth. As long as this cannot be seen there will be the war of sects and religions against each other, and the sending forth of missionaries to insult and irritate, to teach creeds – not Love and Truth. The love of Krishna is deep in the Hindu heart, and cannot be thus slighted with impunity. Yet under all these irritations the Hindu has yet to be found who would retort by any insult or criticism of the founder of Christianity. To the Hindu such criticism of the pure and noble of any race or age is a dreadful crime, involving far-reaching retributive effects. It is a pity we do not think the same.

"One (shepherdess), as she sallied forth, beheld some of the seniors (of the family) and dared not venture, contenting herself with meditating on Krishna with closed eyes and entire devotion, by which, immediately, all acts of merit were effaced by rapture, and all sin was expiated by regret at not beholding Him; and others, again, reflecting upon the cause of the world, in the form of the Supreme Brahma, obtained by their sighing final emancipation." (Vishnu Purana Book V, Chap. XIII, trans. Wilson.)

Both Narada and Sandilya reinstate the allegory in its proper light, the former taking it as an example of his own definition of Love, as … " feeling the greatest misery in forgetting God."

Love has been divided threefold in the Commentary on Sutras 7-14. The love of paramours, always selfish, finds its place under the first or second of these headings.

25. Love is greater than work, knowledge, or Yoga.

26. Because it is its own end.

27. And because Iswara [the personal god] hates pride and loves meekness.

28. Some say Knowledge, indeed, is the means to Love.

29. Others say Love and Knowledge are interdependent.

30. The sons of Brahma (Narada and Sanatkumara) say that Love is its own reward.

31. As is seen in the case of a palace, food, etc.

32. By that there is neither satisfaction to the king nor cessation of hunger.

33. Therefore Love alone is to be embraced by those who desire liberation.

Narada claims that Love is greater than work, knowledge, or yoga, and gives as his reason that it is its own end, not merely a means to an end, as he maintains knowledge is. We have a proverb – "Virtue is its own reward," Narada says the same of Love.

When a king sees a palace he knows then of its existence, but does not by that knowledge become happy, for he does not possess it. So also in the case of a hungry man: the becoming aware of the presence of food does not satisfy him. We need not go into a long disquisition upon such a point, it is merely the rivalry of those who follow the path of Love (Bhakti-marga) and those who follow the path of Wisdom (Jnana-marga). He who has wisdom overflows with Love: he who loves fully overflows with the deepest Wisdom. The path of Love is generally considered the easier, for it acts upon the heart direct: so also does Wisdom, but it may be confused with mere intellectuality. A man may become caught in the snare of the head – the most hopeless and difficult form of ignorance.

Man's progress depends upon the emancipation of the heart. All else is incidental. The heart is the seat of self-ishness in all its forms. The head may work out the most lucid and elaborate of schemes for salvation from misery: may have an explanation for itself of every phenomenon in the universe, yet the heart may remain dark and unilluminated by any proportionate ray of either Love or Wisdom.

The heart is perfectly satisfied that the intellect should amuse itself as long as it does not interfere with heart's dominion, for the intellect always exists as the hench-man of the heart. The struggles of the intellect are entirely with intellectual problems, with cause and sequence in some form. The heart's struggles are with the emotions and desires, and for this purpose it needs the light of the intellect. But often the selfish heart never calls for any light; it makes no move, and however strong the light at its disposal makes no use of it. This state may become habitual, and that life becomes almost stationary as far as reaching the bliss of absolution is concerned.

Only when some great agony or disaster comes which threatens complete disruption of all the desired associations with which the heart has surrounded itself, does this selfish heart call in the intellect to help it in this problem. So far having only used it as the minister of its pleasures, it now needs it to help it to save itself from misery.

Love and Wisdom fight, as it were, for the throne of the heart. Their enemies are Desire and Ignorance. The heart sometimes falls out with its own servant, the Intellect; and through this, Love or Wisdom may gain ground by enlisting one or the other on their side. Their ultimate victory is assured; for the law of remorseless suffering ever presses from behind, and changeless peace and happiness are ever held out in front as the terms of complete surrender.

"Iswara hates pride and loves meekness" – is interesting, as showing the form, which the abstract proposition takes for those who see a Deity into whose likes and dislikes these qualities of meekness and pride are divided. It is seen by all men that pride is to be avoided. The reasons are made to accord with the basic views of the problem of the world which may be held.

34. The teachers thus sing the means of reaching it (Love).

35. By giving up sense objects and worldly company.

36. And by unbroken devotion.

37. In the world also by repeating and hearing the praise of Bhagavan (God).

38. But principally through the compassion of the great, or by a spark of Divine mercy.

39. The company of the great is hard to get, hard to reach, and never in vain.

40. It is obtained through the compassion of God.

41. Because of the absence of difference between Divinity and his own. (We gain Love through the company of the great.)

42. Practise it alone, practise it alone.

Frequenting the society of good and holy men has always been considered a help to pure life. Even where no word is understood of a conversation, the poor and the ignorant to-day in India will come and sit for hours in the company of those they consider holy or exemplary in their lives, watching the expressions of features and actions, and going away respectfully with the impression of these in their hearts. We need to do something more than merely associate with the good and great: we need to make our hearts as theirs: they are "hard to get" for they are difficult to find, and when found are "hard to reach" indeed. To reach them is to become as they, is to admire with a devotion near akin to worship, and which makes us tune our lives by these exemplars. And why should we not worship them? Are they not manifestations of truth? Is it not truth we seek and worship ever? From the dualist's standpoint they are lamps set up by the mercy of God for the guidance of our feet. For the non-dualist they are modifications of truth, manifesting for him within his own mind, and his aspiration is to merge himself with them on his way to absorption in the Great Ocean of Truth.

There is no difference between the will of Divinity and those who have identified their wills with that Divine will; they speak, as it were, with the voice of God. We gain Love, therefore, through these Lovers greater than ourselves. Nothing is so infectious as Love; it is impossible long to resist those who love us disinterestedly. We are fired with their love.

43. In every way bad company is to be abandoned.

44. Because it causes passion, wrath, folly, distraction, loss of decision and loss of energy.

45. These (propensities) being at first like ripples become like oceans.

Care must be taken to discriminate between associating with evil companions in order to take part in their pleasures and trying to better by association those who seem to have fallen into ways producing further ignorance and misery. The teaching of Love is far removed from exclusiveness, for it makes no distinction anywhere. Its method is universal sympathy and patience. Self-righteousness is a very fatal because it is a very subtle poison. So also is over-confidence, which makes a man think he can do anything because he has no longer any attachment, any risk of really falling into bondage. Both are seated in vanity and bring about cruel and remorseless sequences. A cruelty and remorselessness which at length we know as friends, for only through them would we be taught.

46. Who, indeed, crosses Maya (illusion)? He who gives up (evil) company; he who associates with those of great minds; he who becomes without sense of possession.

47. He who frequents lonely places, he who uproots the bondages of the world, goes beyond the three powers (gunas) and abandons all anxiety as to livelihood:

48. He who gives up the fruits of work, abandons all work, and thus becomes freed from the "opposites":

49. He who gives up even the Vedas and attains to unfaltering Love:

50. He crosses, indeed; he crosses and helps others to cross (Maya).

Maya signifies for the bhakta or devotee the bondage of matter through sense attractions and selfishness. The first statement, which is not a repetition of what has gone before, is that he who would cross beyond bondage must abandon all sense of possession. Love has nothing of its own. Wealth, strength, abilities – all must be held only as a trust for the world: as at the service of every striving manifestation of Life.

The true "lonely place" is in the depths of the heart, where with all the doorways to interruption through the senses fastened, he sees there, in unbroken solitude, "One without a second." How are these doorways through which distractions enter to be closed? For the bhakta, through Love, and Love, and yet again Love; by driving everything from his thoughts but sympathy, compassion, and those ideas and emotions that, as it were, lead up to a perfectly impassioned Love – quixotic it may be – reckless, ridiculous to us in its fervour, but unconquerable and unrelenting. Giving it full play, never checking it, weeping it may be for the miseries of the world and the sense of separation from the one Ocean of Life and Love, day and night, in public or in solitude, caring for nothing but attaining the realisation of That: chastising himself through remorse and reproach for every shortcoming in Love, at length he reaches a great calm, a great serenity: he stands on "the other shore." He knows, he feels: his shoulders may become marked with the stripes that fall on those of others, but he suffers no longer: he is ever happy and satisfied. No words can explain that state, and because it cannot be expressed, except by negations, it is a mystery – "The Peace which passeth all understanding."

The three powers, gunas, are the three divisions into which everything in the world falls, according to whether its nature be that of "goodness," "passion," or "inertia." It is the enumeration of the Sankhya-philosophy. The "opposites," of course, are heat and cold, pleasure and pain, praise and blame, etc., etc. One of the greatest signs of Love is the giving up the rewards arising from our efforts, even to that of the attainment of bliss extending over long periods in any heaven. He who has visited a country does not need to read guidebooks. He who has found a reality needs no scriptures. He who advances towards the realization of Love carries along with him by his efforts everybody with whom he comes in contact.

51. Inexpressible is the essential nature of Love (prema).

52. Like the taste of a dumb man.

53. In some particular vessel it makes itself manifest.

54. Devoid of the three qualities, without desires, ever increasing, continuous, having the nature of subtle perception.

55. Having obtained Love he sees that alone, hears that alone, speaks that alone, and thinks that alone.

No religious system pretends to define Deity: it can at the best strive with other systems to suspend some intellectual or emotional veil through which, in shining, the light may take form. Love is one of these, and care is taken to remark that the essential nature of Love, which is that of Deity, cannot be expressed. Like a dumb man who can taste, but cannot express his sense impression. So is Love; it can be felt but not described. It is seen to shine forth in some particular individual (lit.: "vessel"). It is found to be free of the three qualities or powers which are inherent in all material things (sattwa, rajas and tamas – brightness or goodness, action or passion, and inertia or stupidity); it has no selfishness, it seems ever to grow greater the more it is sought; it never falters; it is found in the heart as a subtlety by those who centre their keenest perceptions inwardly. Once having experienced Love, all a man's activities become devoted to it.

56. Worshippers are threefold, according to the three qualities, or divided according to supplicant, etc.

57. The first of the three is higher than the other two in either group.

The description of various forms of worship and different worshippers can be found in the Bhagavad Gita. The three qualities have already been named: "supplicant," etc., stands for inquirer or seeker of worldly prosperity also. Of these, he who devotes himself to the "brightness" (or goodness) quality in himself, and he who is a supplicant (that divine compassion and Love may become visible for him) are the two foremost.

"Four kinds of good men worship me, Arjuna, the afflicted, he who seeks knowledge, he who desires gain, and the wise."

"At the end of many births, the man possessed of wisdom comes to me, but that Mahatma (great souled one) who says 'Vasudeva is All' is very hard to find." (Bh. Gita, VII, 16, 19)

58. Love (bhakti) is easier than other methods.

59. Being self-evident it does not depend on other truths.

60. And from being of the nature of peace and supreme bliss.

These verses have already found an explanation in the remarks on verses 25-33.

61. Destruction of popular usages is not to be thought of. Consecrated souls paying respect to social and scriptural usages.

62. When Love has been attained, social customs are not to be scorned, but they are to be performed (giving up the fruits).

There is a great tendency when the mind has become free to forget the guiding forms that are necessary for others, who are still bound by prejudices, ignorance or selfishness. An opinion tends to form that it is hypocritical to conform outwardly where inwardly we recognise only a custom or a form, and that we can forcibly tear off the bandages from the eyes of others. There is a difference in the limitation of Truth which still, however, directs people in the right direction, and a distortion or perversion. Truth is limited for every manifested being, and it is always only a question of degree. Out of this subtle question has arisen a host of intellectual quibbles, and amongst them that of justifying the means by the end. We have the advocate of breaking down everything he has passed beyond himself, and his rival who maintains that the motive alone counts and that methods are nothing, that any false hope can be nurtured in another, any deception practised if it leads the votary in the right direction.

The answer to all this is that there are certain forms and observances which lead to less disguised truths, which make a ladder by the steps of which men may mount, and there are other methods again which are extremely indirect or opposite in direction to the above. Of these two sets, a man should follow in observance what he deems to lead in the right direction, and oppose all that is contrary to it or extremely indirect. For him who has "gone beyond the opposites," "good and evil" are mere names; yet if he, whilst living amongst men, did not conform to what they can see as good and avoid what they can see as evil he would be kicking down the long ladder by which he himself, through ages of faithful recognition and belief in good and evil, had mounted.

63. Descriptions of woman's beauty, atheistical writings, and the doings of the enemies of Love are not to be listened to.

64. Egotism and arrogance are to be abandoned.

65. Surrendering all activities to Him, even passion, wrath and pride, etc., are to be employed in that (connection only).

The most effective way to become free of any bondage, whether that of passion ("woman's beauty"), or the wish to ridicule or revile (scurrilous literature), or wrath, indignation and violence (the doings of the enemies of Love), is to abstract the mind from such tendencies, and fix it upon something else. Listening to and talking of these things only implants seeds in the mind which may germinate.

"For expelling a doubtful subject (practise) pondering upon its opposite." (Patanjali)

Verse 65 seems strange. Supposing a man to have passion, wrath and pride so strong that he cannot subdue them, then let him try to fix his passion in an intense devotion to God as the Beautiful and Perfect. If he has wrath, let him pour it out upon himself, upon his own shortcomings. If he has pride, let him be proud of his "friendship" with God, that God is his Lover. So in time these weaknesses become gradually transmuted.

66. Merging the three in one by regarding oneself as eternal servant or eternal beloved. Love (prema) is to be given.

67. Those worshippers who have this one object in life are the greatest.

68. With choking voice and hair standing on end, and with tears, talking to each other of Love, they purify their families in the world.

69. They are the source of holiness to holy places. They make any work good work, and Scriptures Holy Scriptures.

70. They are full of Divinity.

71. Their forefathers rejoice. The Gods dance with joy. This earth finds protectors.

72. Amongst them no distinction is to be made of caste, learning, beauty, birth, wealth, occupation, etc.

73. Because they are His.

The three are Lover, Love, and Beloved. These are to be united in one, so that no separation any longer exists anywhere. Or the bhakta may look upon himself as servant, and by rendering service to all beings, in whom he sees divinity, thus serve God. Or he may feel himself as beloved, and pour out his love in return upon all the works of God – the Lover.

"With choking voice," etc., expresses the highest states of emotion. These are contagious, and their manifestation undoubtedly tends to exalt the hearts of others. In extreme joy the down upon the body is said to stand erect. In Western countries this phenomenon has not been observed, for our bodies are always covered. We feel, however, a peculiar movement of the skin which accompanies deep emotional experiences of a pleasurable sort. There are several references to this movement of the down upon the body in old Sanskrit literature.

Those in whom Love shines perfectly throw a halo of sanctity over everything they do, over everything they touch or approach.

Thought is a great power, a marvellous energy, which surpasses all others in its scope. Marvellous is the rapidity of action and the almost instantaneous work of electricity, but these lag far behind the powers of thought. Thought can build and destroy: it works through every manifestation in this universe.

"The whole world verily is mind."

Through its subtlety it evades: its very methods raise in us the idea that we alone are the thinkers of our thoughts. Whence rise the motives, whence the suggestions that play upon the strings of our hearts, which pulsate in our brains from hour to hour, day to day? Who can sink so deep into the promptings that move as to discover even their approximate origin? Yet we identify them all with the basic conception "I." He who, maybe, sits in a cave or apparently idles away life in the sunshine, who undertakes no works through the pen or through the purse, who, apparently, has no part in practical efforts to benefit, may, nevertheless, be a living battery from which radiates in every direction powerful influence in the shape of thought. Pure and selfless, it may vibrate through the world and stimulate and encourage the minds that are in accord with it. Higher than the poets, beyond the essayist or preacher, is he who can understand, control and project ideas. There can be no resistance to what cannot be seen, except by its like – by thought.

The same law applies to evil suggestions and to good. These are everywhere, and minds feed upon them for weal or for woe according to their necessity. The very walls of old sanctuaries and rooms where the blessed and the pure have lived are impregnated with their thought. This may last for centuries. It can only be known and felt by those who are receptive to such influences, and they are very rare. For to have read the life of a saint, to have filled oneself with his written teaching, and then to visit the scene of his labours, brings into play other factors.

The forefathers rejoice, and the gods are elated with joy, for they see, in anticipation, their own victory, their own relief from bondage. Man is the highest of all the manifestations in the universe; for it is only through human birth that identity with God can be obtained, and final release from the bondage of birth, growth, decay, and death. All the gods in the highest heavens are subject to these, nor can they pass by any other portal to Moksha – to release – except through human birth.

Hence, when Christ conquered, the angels came and ministered to Him, and so also do they rejoice and serve every man who becomes a Christ. From the highest heavens to the nethermost hells the worlds "trembled" when Buddha conquered, for his is the victory which frees for ever. It is the basic hope of every living thing, seated deep within its heart, and unknown to itself, except in the case of men and gods. By such victories, only possible through manhood, the foundations of all the manifested worlds are shaken. On the occasion of the victories both of Christ and Buddha there were "mighty earthquakes". By slow or by quicker stages every living thing passes through humanity, through Christhood, or Buddhahood, into God.

When a man has obtained the condition of a perfect bhakta he no longer manifests, as it were, humanity. He reflects Divinity direct. He speaks with the voice of God. Distinctions of caste, learning, etc., are no longer possible.

74. Vain discussions are to be avoided.

75. Because of their immensity and uncertainty.

76. Devotional Scriptures are to be pondered over, and works that increase devotion should be performed.

Discussion is either destructive or constructive. The former is "vain." Leave others their theories and systems: be satisfied with building and expressing your own. Work upon those books which develop your own idiosyncrasies – in this case bhakti, Love.

77. Abandoning pleasure and pain, longing, seeking for gain, etc., leaving these to time, do not spend half a moment in vain.

78. Harmlessness, truthfulness, purity, mercy, affirming the truths of Scripture, these virtues should be observed.

79. Always with full concentration and without any anxiety, God is to be worshipped.

80. Being praised, He manifests Himself soon and makes Himself felt by His worshippers.

81. In all times (past, present and future) Love is the greatest thing.

Seek no means but Love, and do not delay. Pleasure and pain, restless seeking and all the rest are to be left for time to work upon. Cause and effect are inevitable in the world of thought, as elsewhere. The wheel revolves after the propelling hand is withdrawn. All causes which lie within us biding their time must inevitably be worked out, but the effects may not "stain" us, may not affect us, if we have become entirely without "attachment to the fruit of works." If a mother left alone in the world to protect her babe can so ignore disease and pain as to prolong her life for the sake of her child over many years, and many such cases are known, how much more is this the case with him whose attention is now given more and more to God!

Even to-day there are those who decline medical assistance when suffering from fever, dysentery and the like. "These are effects of the past," say they, "let them work themselves out as they may. Our attention is wholly with God."

Those are the most hopeless patients for doctors who pity themselves, whose thoughts are always about themselves. The same morbid processes may be applied to the mind, and lead to untold misery. We find everywhere in the world those are the happiest who have forgotten themselves in their devotion to some other object. If, when the object is even material and transient, it can thus produce happiness (equally transient though it be) how much more is this the case where the object, besides being eternal, ever appears to grow more satisfying!

Therefore the bhakta should be "without any anxieties." He takes the Love of God; he gives all he has, feeling that that too is God's Love returning to itself. There is no Love in the query, "Am I saved?" But compare the following:

"O Lord! O Imperishable One! In whatever thousands of births I may wonder, may my undying love be always in Thee." (Vishnu Purana)

There is Divine Love already in the heart that aspires thus, and as verse 80 says, "He manifests Himself soon, and makes Himself felt by His worshippers."

82. Attachment through glory. Attachment through duty. Attachment through worship. Attachment as a servant. Attachment as friend. Attachment as beloved. Attachment as a child. Attachment as self-sacrifice. Attachment by identification. Attachment by misery in separation (as in the case of lovers). Thus the one Love takes eleven modes.

There are an almost infinite number of methods in yoga. Each mind must choose according to its idiosyncrasy. "Attachment to glory" is by wonder and admiration of power, grandeur, etc., as manifested in the universe." "Through beauty" is the aesthetic method, through art, etc. All forms are beautiful as displaying the work of the Lover. "Through worship" explains itself, as do the rest. By "misery and separation" is through finding happiness only when God is remembered, when He is, as it were, present in the heart, and through feeling that all is desolate when in looking out upon the objective transient worlds that One Eternal is forgotten.

83. Thus say Kumara, Vyasa, Suka, Sandilya, Garga, Vishnu, Sesa, Udhava, Varuni, Bali, Hanuman, Vibhisana, etc., who were teachers of Love (*bhakti*), and who were fearless whether what they said was considered prattle or wisdom.

84. He who believes and reveres this declared by Narada, by the command of Siva, he becomes possessed of Love, he gains that Dearest.

The names of Sages given here are the names of those who gave rise to various lines of doctrinal descent. They all taught in one way or another what has been declared in these verses. This line of descent from teacher to disciple, who in his turn becomes teacher and hands down to a disciple, goes on through ages and is deemed of great importance. It is known as guruparampara. The thoughts and words of a sage go on echoing and re-echoing through the world for ages: more especially in the hearts of those who by initiation (diksha) stand in sympathy with that teaching. True teachers of Christ are in the guruparampara of Christ. With

His words (which have nothing to do with language merely) is handed down such portion of the irresistible spiritual will of the Great and Pure Teacher as the modern day exponent may be able to find in himself. So also with the true followers of Buddha, the teachers of the Good Law. So also with those who have "taken diksha" in any of the lines of descent mentioned in the verse. This taking diksha does not limit a man, does not prevent him thinking for himself or learning through other teachers, but there is deemed to come down to him a special influence, a wave of the spiritual thought of the ancient teacher (guru), kept alive and perhaps increased by those through whom it has come.

Vivekananda: Lecture on Narada Bhakti Sutras in Thousand Island Park

(Vivekananda: Inspired Talks, 24. June 1895: Complete Works VII)

"Extreme love to God is Bhakti, and this love is the real immortality, getting which a man becomes perfectly satisfied, sorrows for no loss, and is never jealous; knowing which man becomes mad."

My Master [Ramakrishna] used to say, "This world is a huge lunatic asylum where all men are mad, some after money, some after women, some after name or fame, and a few after God. I prefer to be mad after God. God is the philosophers' stone that turns us to gold in an instant; the form remains, but the nature is changed – the human form remains, but no more can we hurt or sin."

"Thinking of God, some weep, some sing, some laugh, some dance, some say wonderful things, but all speak of nothing but God."

Prophets preach, but the Incarnations like Jesus, Buddha, Ramakrishna, can give religion; one glance, one touch is enough. That is the power of the Holy Ghost, the "laying on of hands"; the power was actually transmitted to the disciples by the Master – the "chain of

Guru-power". That, the real baptism, has been handed down for untold ages.

"Bhakti cannot be used to fulfil any desires, itself being the check to all desires." Narada gives these as the signs of love: "When all thoughts, all words, and all deeds are given up unto the Lord, and the least forgetfulness of God makes one intensely miserable, then love has begun."

"This is the highest form of love because therein is no desire for reciprocity, which desire is in all human love."

"A man who has gone beyond social and scriptural usage, he is a Sannyasin. When the whole soul goes to God, when we take refuge only in God, then we know that we are about to get this love."

Obey the scriptures until you are strong enough to do without them; then go beyond them. Books are not an end-all. Verification is the only proof of religious truth. Each must verify for himself; and no teacher who says, "I have seen, but *you* cannot", is to be trusted, only that one who says, "You can see too". All scriptures, all truths are Vedas in all times, in all countries; because these truths are to be *seen*, and any one may discover them.

"When the sun of Love begins to break on the horizon, we want to give up all our actions unto God; and when we forget Him for a moment, it grieves us greatly."

Let nothing stand between God and your love for Him. Love Him, love Him, love Him; and let the world say what it will. Love is of three sorts one demands, but gives nothing; the second is exchange; and the third is love without thought of return – love like that of the moth for the light.

"Love is higher than work, than Yoga, than knowledge."

Work is merely a schooling for the doer; it can do no good to others. We must work out our own problem; the prophets only show us how to work. "What you think, you become", so if you throw your burden on Jesus, you will have to think of Him and thus become like Him – you *love* Him.

"Extreme love and highest knowledge are one."

But theorising about God will not do; we must love and work. Give up the world and all worldly things, especially while the "plant" is tender. Day and night think of God and think of nothing else as far as possible. The daily necessary thoughts can all be thought through God. Eat to Him, drink to Him, sleep to Him, see Him in all. Talk of God to others; this is most beneficial.

Get the mercy of God and of His greatest children: these are the two chief ways to God. The company of these children of light is very hard to get; five minutes in their company will change a whole life; and if you really want it enough, one will come to you. The presence of those who love God makes a place holy, "such is the glory of the children of the Lord". They are He; and when they speak, their words are scriptures. The place where they have been becomes filled with their vibrations, and those going there feel them and have a tendency to become holy also.

"To such lovers there is no distinction of caste, learning, beauty, birth, wealth, or occupation; because all are His."

Give up all evil company, especially at the beginning. Avoid worldly company, that will distract your mind. Give up all "me and mine". To him who has nothing in the universe the Lord comes. Cut the bondage of all worldly affections; go beyond laziness and all care as to what becomes of you. Never turn back to see the result of what you have done. Give all to the Lord and go on and think not of it. The whole soul pours in a continuous current to God; there is no time to seek money, or name, or fame, no time to think of anything but God; then will come into our hearts that infinite, wonderful bliss of Love. All desires are but beads of glass. Love of God increases every moment and is ever new, to be known only by feeling it. Love is the easiest of all, it waits for no logic, it is natural. We need no demonstration, no proof. Reasoning is limiting something by our own minds. We throw a net and catch something, and then say that we have demonstrated it; but never, never can we catch God in a net.

Love should be unrelated. Even when we love wrongly, it is of the true love, of the true bliss; the power is the same, use it as we may. Its very nature is peace and bliss. The murderer when he kisses his baby forgets for an instant all but love. Give up all self, all egotism and get out of anger, lust, give all to God. "I am not, but Thou art; the old man is all gone, only Thou remainest." "I am Thou." Blame none; if evil comes, know the Lord is playing with you and be exceeding glad.

Love is beyond time and space, it is absolute.